D0021843
P9-DGC-414

FAST! JET PLANES

... and other fast machines in the air

QEB
QEB Publishing

IAN GRAHAM

The words in **bold** are explained in the Glossary on page 30.

***Front cover:* The Russian MiG-29 is one of the world's leading supersonic fighters (see page 18).**

Project Editor: Angela Royston
Designer: Andrew Crowson
Picture Researcher: Maria Joannou

Published in the United States by
QEB Publishing, Inc.
3 Wrigley, Suite A
Irvine, CA 92618

www.qed-publishing.co.uk

Library of Congress Cataloging-in-Publication Data

Graham, Ian, 1953-
Jet planes / Ian Graham.
p. cm. -- (Fast!)
Includes bibliographical references and index.
ISBN 978-1-59566-928-5 (library binding : alk. paper)
1. Jet planes--Juvenile literature. 2. Aeronautics--Records--Juvenile literature. 3. Airplanes--Speed records--Juvenile literature. I. Title.
TR547.G753 2011
779'.93877334--dc22

2010006061

Printed in China

Picture credits
Alamy Images EuroStyle Graphics 14–15, Trinity Mirror/Mirrorpix 8–9, Bernard Friel/Danita Delimont 11t, Imagebroker/Günter Flegar 11c, Barry Bland 11b, UK Alan King 16–17t; **Corbis** Denis Balibouse/Reuters 6t, Jean-Christophe Bott/EPA 6–7, Bettmann 9c, 13t & c, Skyscan 10–11, Smithsonian Institution 15c, Paco Campos/EFE 19t; **Getty Images** AFP/Fabrice Coffrini 7tl, Hulton Archive/Fox Photos/Stringer 8t; **Library of Congress** 4–5, 5b; **NASA** 24, 25tl, tr & b, 26, 27tl & tr, Dryden Flight Research Center 5c, 15t, 20, 21t & b, 22b, 22–23, 23tr, Johnson Space Center Collection 27b, Steve Lighthill 28–29, 29tr; **Photolibrary** Philip Wallick 16–17b; **Reaction Engines Limited** Adrian Mann 29b; **Rex Features** 7r, Rob Judges 16c, Sipa Press 17c; **Scaled Composites, LLC** 23b, Jim Campbell/Aero-News Network 5t; **Shutterstock** perspectives FC, Lars Christensen BC; **Topham Picturepoint** 2006 Alinari 9t, Flight Collection 12t, 19c, Ullsteinbild 12–13; **U.S. Air Force** 18–19, 21c, Senior Airman Vernon Young 18t, Chad Bellay 28b

Note: The planes appear in order of speed, from the slowest to the fastest.

Fastest in the air

The first planes struggled into the air for just a few seconds. Today, there are jet planes that travel faster than sound, and rocket-planes that can fly into space and back.

The first plane

The first plane powered by an engine was called *Flyer*. It was built by two brothers, Orville and Wilbur Wright. In 1903, with Orville at the controls, it flew for just 12 seconds. It was the fastest plane in the world, because it was the only plane in the world!

The *Wright Flyer* takes off for the first-ever powered flight.

Faster and faster

Flyer's success showed that powered flight was possible. Other people then quickly started to build their own planes. As the engines became more powerful, the planes became faster and faster. Pilots raced against each other, and competed to set new air speed records.

In 2004, *SpaceShipOne* flew into space. It flew three times faster than the *X-1*.

The *X-1* flew faster than the speed of sound in 1947.

FACTFILE

Wright Flyer

- Wingspan: 40.3 feet (12.3 meters)
- Engine: Wright engine
- Power: 12 horsepower
- Top speed: 9.8 miles per hour (15.7 kilometers per hour)
- Crew: 1

HOW FAST?

The *Wright Flyer* flew about as fast as someone running along the ground.

Jet-man

Swiss pilot Yves Rossy was used to flying fighters and airliners. He also dreamed of flying through the air on his own, like Superman.

Rossy's wing has two jet engines on each side.

Four jets

Rossy had a special wing made using **carbon fiber**. Then he added four **jet engines** of the kind that usually power a large model aircraft. In 2006, he strapped the wing to his back and jumped out of a plane. Then he started the jet engines and flew on his own for the first time.

Rossy jets through the air like a one-man plane.

FACTFILE

Yves Rossy's jet-wing

- Wingspan: 7.9 feet (2.4 meters)
- Engine: Four model aircraft jet engines
- Power: Unknown
- Top speed: 189 miles per hour (304 kilometers per hour)
- Crew: 1

HOW FAST?

With his jet-wing, Yves Rossy can fly as fast as a racing car.

The jet-man returns to the ground by parachute.

Channel crossing

In 2008, Rossy used his jet-wing to fly across the English Channel. He made the crossing in only 9 minutes and reached 125 miles per hour (200 kilometers per hour). Later the same year, he flew over the Alps, a mountain range in Europe, at a top speed of 189 miles per hour (304 kilometers per hour).

Air racers

Air races were very popular in the 1920s and 1930s. They encouraged aircraft designers to produce new, faster, and more advanced planes.

A Supermarine seaplane is prepared for a race.

Seaplane races

The Schneider Trophy air races were for **seaplanes**. They attracted crowds of more than 200,000 people. The last Schneider Trophy race was held in 1931, when the United Kingdom won the trophy for the third time. The winning plane was a Supermarine S.6B with an average speed of 340 miles per hour (547 kilometers per hour).

The Macchi M.C.72 was the fastest plane in 1933 and 1934.

Record breaker

The Italian Macchi M.C.72 racing seaplane was not able to take part in the last Schneider Trophy race, because of engine trouble. But it went on to break the S.6B's air speed record twice. In 1934 it raised the record speed to 411 miles per hour (709 kilometers per hour).

A Supermarine S.6B starts its takeoff run.

FACTFILE

Macchi M.C.72

- Wingspan: 31 feet (9.5 meters)
- Engine: Fiat V24
- Power: 2,850 horsepower
- Top speed: 441 miles per hour (709 kilometers per hour)
- Crew: 1

HOW FAST?

The Macchi M.C.72 was twice as fast as a racing car at top speed.

War planes

No new air speed records were set between 1939 and 1945, because the world was at war. However, faster and faster aircraft were developed during World War II.

Fast fighters

The best fighters for air battles were lightweight and fast. By 1945, some fighters were flying faster than the record-breaking speeds set before the war. The Hawker Hurricane fighter had a top speed of 338 miles per hour (544 kilometers per hour). The famous Spitfire fighter and its rival, the Messerschmitt Bf-109, were even faster.

The Spitfire's top speed was more than 375 miles per hour (600 kilometers per hour).

Flying faster

During World War II, newer planes, such as the P-51D Mustang, were built. They were faster than the Spitfire. Later planes, such as the Corsair navy fighter, were even faster. The Corsair's top speed was about 446 miles per hour (718 kilometers per hour). But the age of fast planes with **propellers** was coming to an end.

Some Mustangs took part in air races after the war.

The Corsair's engine was the most powerful in the world in 1940.

FACTFILE

Vought F4U-4 Corsair

- Wingspan: 41 feet (12.5 meters)
- Engine: Pratt & Whitney R-2800 radial engine
- Power: 2,450 horsepower
- Top speed: 446 miles per hour (718 kilometers per hour)
- Crew: 1

HOW FAST?

At top speed, a Mustang or Corsair fighter could fly the length of two soccer fields in about one second!

First jet fighters

The first jet fighters were built in the 1940s, during World War II. They could fly far faster than planes with propellers.

Jet planes

The jet engine was invented in Britain by Frank Whittle in 1930, but Germany built the first jet plane. The German Heinkel He-178 made the first jet-powered flight on August 27, 1939. Germany also built the first jet fighter, the Messerschmitt Me-262. It had a top speed of 540 miles per hour (870 kilometers per hour). It was much faster than other fighters at that time.

The Heinkel He-178 was the first practical jet plane.

The Me-262 was the first fighter without a propeller.

A Gloster Meteor was the fastest plane in the world in 1945.

New records

The first British jet fighter was the Gloster Meteor. In 1945, a Meteor that had been **modified** to go faster than normal set the first air speed record after the war. It flew at 606 miles per hour (975 kilometers per hour). Air forces in different countries quickly changed from fighters with propellers to jet-powered fighters.

FACTFILE

Gloster Meteor

- Wingspan: 43 feet (13.1 meters)
- Engines: Two Rolls-Royce W.2B/23 Welland turbojets
- Power: 15,100 newtons
- Top speed: 606 miles per hour (975 kilometers per hour)
- Crew: 1

HOW FAST?

The record-breaking Gloster Meteor was as fast as a jet airliner today.

Faster than sound

When pilots flew close to the speed of sound, their planes shook and became harder to steer. There was something strange about the speed of sound that plane-makers struggled to understand.

The sound barrier

Some people thought it might be impossible to fly faster than sound safely, so the **speed of sound** became known as the sound barrier. The first plane to break through the barrier was the *Bell X-1*. It was an **experimental** plane powered by a **rocket.**

The *Bell X-1* was shaped like a bullet.

The Super Sabre was the first U.S. supersonic fighter plane.

Sonic boom

On October 14, 1947, the *X-1* was carried into the air underneath a B-29 bomber. At a height of nearly 20,000 feet (6,000 meters), the bomber dropped the *X-1*. Its pilot, Charles "Chuck" Yeager, fired the rocket and the plane soared away. As the *X-1* went through the sound barrier, people on the ground heard a loud sonic boom. Supersonic (faster than sound) flight had arrived!

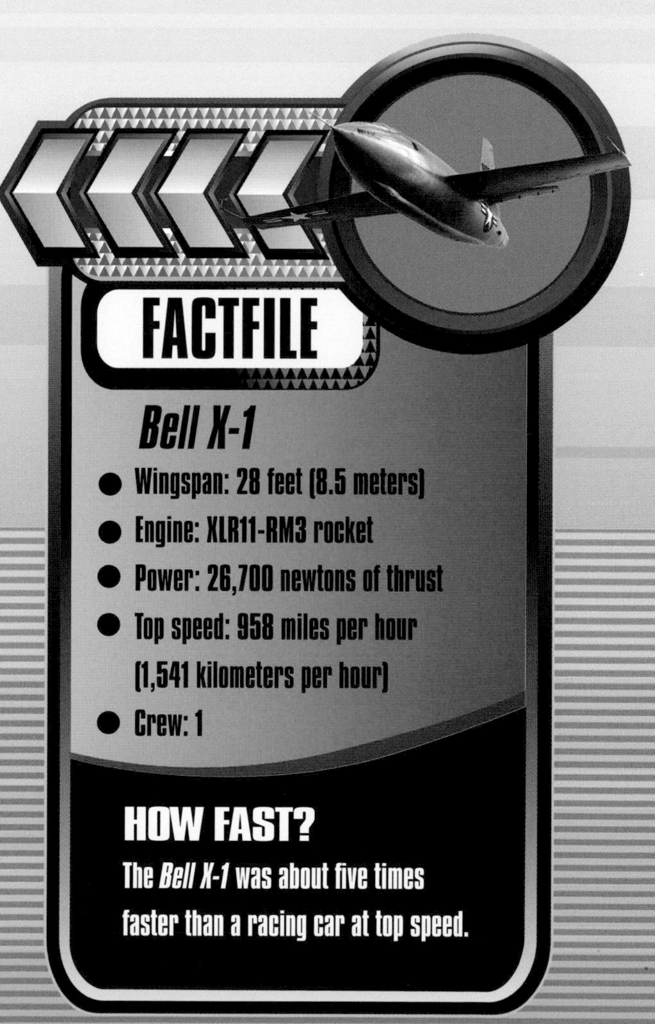

Concorde

In the 1950s, Britain and France started work on a new supersonic plane. It was to be a supersonic airliner, and it was called Concorde.

Concorde's nose was lowered to give a better view for landing.

Concorde could out-fly most military jets, because it could fly at supersonic speeds for several hours.

Working together

At first, Britain and France worked separately on different airliners. Later, they joined forces and worked together on the same project. They built a slender, white, dart-shaped plane. Concorde made its first test-flight on March 2, 1969. It went supersonic seven months later, and carried its first paying passengers on January 21, 1976.

Concorde flew at a height of 11 miles (18 kilometers) above the ground.

Faster flights

Concorde **cruised** at just over twice the speed of sound. It halved the time for a flight across the Atlantic Ocean, and it flew nearly twice as high as other airliners. Concorde flights stopped in 2000, after the aircraft's only crash. They began again in 2001, but all Concorde flights ended for good two years later. It cost too much money to keep the plane flying.

FACTFILE

Concorde

- Wingspan: 84 feet (25.6 meters)
- Engines: Four Olympus 593 jet engines
- Power: 676,000 newtons of thrust
- Top speed: 1,355 miles per hour (2,180 kilometers per hour)
- Crew: 3

HOW FAST?

Concorde could fly from London, U.K., to New York, a distance of 3,470 miles (5,580 kilometers), in about 3 hours.

Supersonic fighters

The first supersonic fighters were built in the 1950s. Today, fighters can easily fly at more than twice the speed of sound. They are about 150 times faster than the first airplane!

The Raptor is named after fierce birds of prey.

The fighting Raptor

The Lockheed Martin F-22 Raptor is the latest U.S. fighter. It began its service with the U.S. Air Force in 2005. Its top speed is just over twice the speed of sound. Planes like the F-22 are amazingly expensive. Each F-22 costs more than $100 million.

The F-22 Raptor has two jet engines.

Europe's fighter

The latest European fighter is the Eurofighter Typhoon. The first Typhoon was delivered to the German Air Force in 2003. Six air forces now have Typhoons. Plane-makers in Germany, the U.K., and Italy worked together to create the Typhoon. It has a top speed of nearly 1,550 miles per hour (2,500 kilometers per hour). Tiny **swiveling** wings on the plane's nose help it to turn more tightly in air battles.

A Typhoon can weigh up to 23.5 tons.

FACTFILE

Eurofighter Typhoon

- Wingspan: 35.9 feet (10.95 meters)
- Engines: Two Eurojet EJ200 turbofans
- Power: 120,000 newtons of thrust
- Top speed: 1,550 miles per hour (2,495 kilometers per hour)
- Crew: 1

HOW FAST?

The Eurofighter Typhoon is more than twice as fast as an airliner.

Blackbird

In 1976, a plane called the Lockheed SR-71 Blackbird flew at 2,193 miles per hour (3,529 kilometers per hour). This air speed record for manned jet planes has never been broken.

Spy in the sky

The Blackbird was a U.S. Air Force spy-plane. It flew so high and so fast that no enemy plane or **missile** could catch it. Its strange flattened shape and special black paint protected it, too. They were chosen to make the plane harder for an enemy to find by using **radar**. It flew thousands of secret missions from 1964 to 1998.

The Blackbird's nose contains spy cameras.

The Blackbird's tail fins lean inward.

High flyer

The Blackbird flew at more than three times the speed of sound. It flew up to about 85,000 feet (25,900 meters)—more than twice as high as an ordinary airliner. In fact, it flew so high that the two crew members had to wear spacesuits. The Blackbird has now been replaced by spy **satellites** in space.

High-flying Blackbird pilots wore spacesuits.

FACTFILE

Lockheed SR-71 Blackbird

- Wingspan: 55.4 feet (16.9 meters)
- Engines: Two Pratt & Whitney J58 jet engines
- Power: 290,000 newtons of thrust
- Top speed: 2,193 miles per hour (3,529 kilometers) per hour
- Crew: 2

HOW FAST?

The Blackbird flew four times faster than an airliner.

Edge of space

Twenty years before the Space Shuttle started carrying astronauts into orbit in 1981, a rocket-plane was already flying into space. It was an experimental rocket-plane called the *X-15*.

Soaring away

The *X-15* could fly more than six times faster than sound, but it never held the world air speed record. To set a new record, an aircraft has to be able to take off by itself. The *X-15* was carried into the air underneath the wing of a B-52 bomber. The bomber dropped the *X-15* at a height of 44,950 feet (13,700 meters). Then the pilot fired the *X-15*'s rocket and soared away.

The *X-15* made a total of 199 flights.

The *X-15* was carried into the air by a bomber.

The *X-15* was powered by a rocket in its tail.

FACTFILE

North American X-15

- Wingspan: 22.3 feet (6.8 meters)
- Engine: Thiokol XLR99-RM-2 rocket
- Power: 310,000 newtons of thrust
- Top speed: 4,520 miles per hour (7,274 kilometers per hour)
- Crew: 1

HOW FAST?

The *X-15* flew eight times faster than an airliner.

SpaceShipOne

In 2004, another rocket-plane dropped from a **mothership** flew to the edge of space. It was called *SpaceShipOne*. It was the first manned spacecraft developed by a private company, not a government agency. Its top speed was about 2,200 miles per hour (3,500 kilometers per hour).

SpaceShipOne hangs below its mothership.

Space Shuttle

The Space Shuttle is nearly four times faster than the *X-15*. It has to reach a speed of about 17,400 miles per hour (28,000 kilometers per hour) to go into orbit around Earth.

The Space Shuttle blasts off from its launch pad.

Boosting power

When the Space Shuttle takes off, the Orbiter vehicle with the astronauts inside is attached to two booster rockets and a huge tank of fuel. The fuel is burned by the three rocket engines in the Orbiter's tail. The engines and boosters provide the power needed to launch the Shuttle.

The Space Shuttle soars away from Earth.

Around Earth

When the fuel is used up, the fuel tank and booster rockets fall away. The Orbiter carries on into orbit around Earth. At the end of its mission, the Orbiter slips out of orbit and returns to Earth. It re-enters the atmosphere at about 25 times the speed of sound.

The Orbiter lands like a plane on a runway.

Apollo 10

The fastest craft ever to fly through the air with a crew was the command module of the *Apollo 10* space mission.

Moon mission

The *Apollo 10* spacecraft orbited the Moon two months before *Apollo 11* landed the first astronauts on the Moon. *Apollo 10*'s job was to practice everything that *Apollo 11* would do, except land on the Moon. The spacecraft was made up of three parts—the command **module**, the service module, and the lunar excursion module. Only the command module landed back on Earth. The spacecraft was launched by a mighty *Saturn V* rocket, which was as powerful as 130 jet fighters.

The giant *Saturn V* rocket was as tall as a 36-story skyscraper.

The Apollo spacecraft orbits the Moon.

FACTFILE

Apollo 10

- Wingspan: None
- Engines: 11 rocket engines of the Saturn V launcher
- Power: 40 million newtons of thrust
- Top speed: 24,791 miles per hour (39,897 kilometers per hour)
- Crew: 3

HOW FAST?

Apollo 10's command module flew more than 100 times faster than a racing car.

The pull of gravity

As *Apollo 10* returned to Earth, the pull of Earth's **gravity** made it fly faster and faster. Astronauts Thomas Stafford, John Young, and Eugene Cernan were inside the tiny spacecraft. As it plunged into the atmosphere, the command module was traveling at nearly 25,000 miles per hour (40,000 kilometers) per hour!

The *Apollo 10* Command Module landed in the ocean.

Future records

Aircraft that fly faster than five times the speed of sound are called hypersonic. Future hypersonic aircraft are being designed now.

Test flight

Some hypersonic aircraft will be able to fly 10 or even 20 times faster than the speed of sound. A small **unmanned** plane called the *X-51* will make test flights up to about seven times the speed of sound. Another unmanned aircraft called *X-43A* has already reached almost 10 times the speed of sound. It was fitted to a rocket hanging underneath a B-52 bomber. The bomber launched the rocket. Then the *X-43A*'s engine started and the plane soared away.

The *X-51* and its rocket are prepared for a flight.

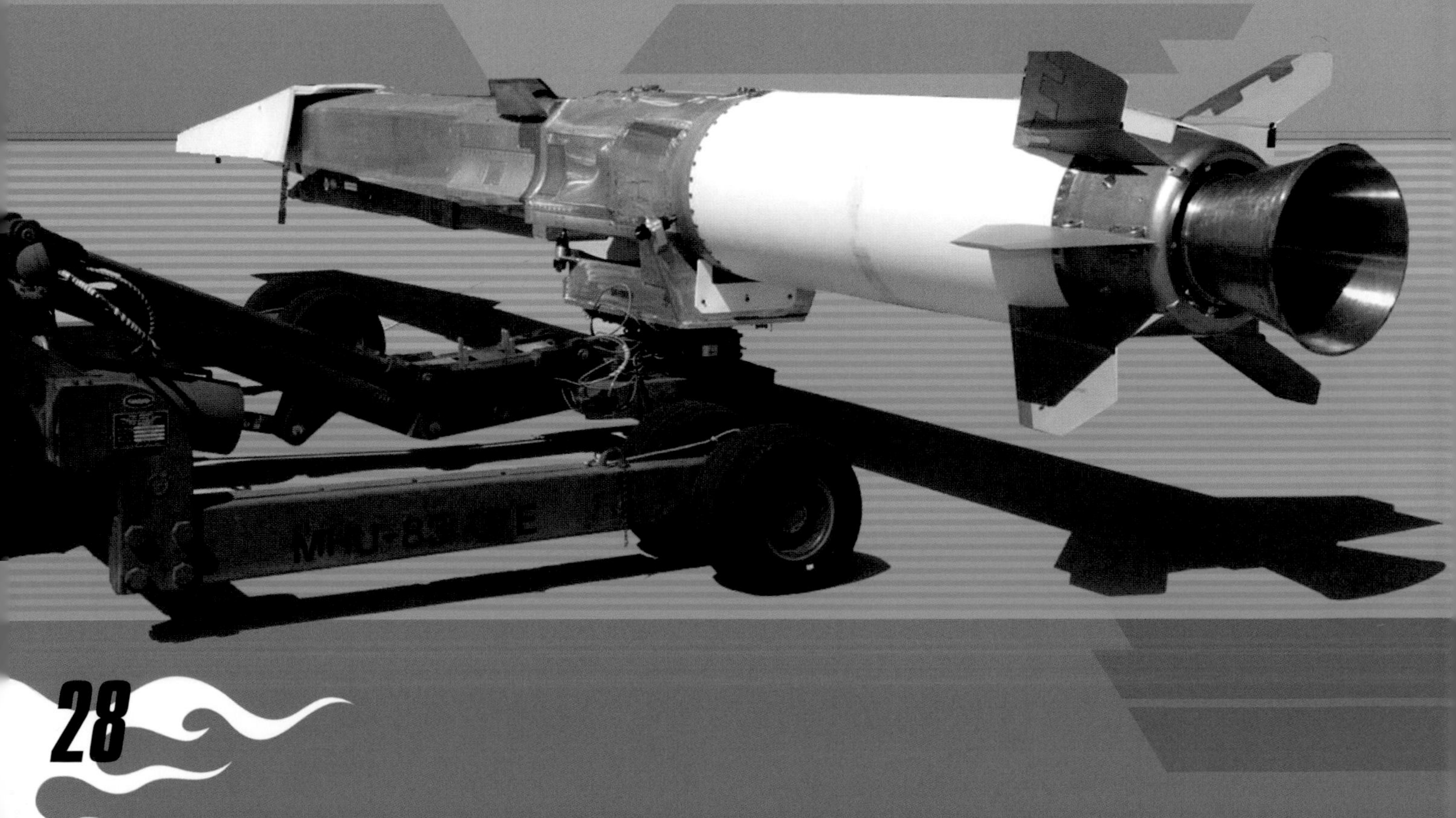

A small model *X-43* has made three test flights.

FACTFILE

X-43A

- Wingspan: 5 feet (1.5 meters)
- Engine: Scramjet engine
- Power: Unknown
- Top speed: 7,000 miles per hour (11,265 kilometers per hour)
- Crew: None

HOW FAST?

A plane flying at ten times the speed of sound would travel from New York to Tokyo in less than two hours, a flight that normally takes about 14 hours today.

Hypersonic airliner

A hypersonic airliner called the A2 is being designed in Britain. If it is built, it will carry 300 passengers at five times the speed of sound. A plane like this could fly from western Europe to Australia in less than five hours, a flight that takes about 23 hours today.

The A2 is a future hypersonic airliner.

Glossary

carbon fiber A very strong, lightweight material made from plastic, strengthened by strands of carbon.

cruised Flew at the speed that burned the smallest amount of fuel.

experimental Built specially to test something new, such as a new shape of aircraft or a new type of engine, or to set a record.

gravity A force that pulls everything down toward the ground. Planes have to overcome gravity to get off the ground and fly.

jet engine An engine that produces a fast stream of hot air to push a plane along. The air is heated by burning fuel inside the engine.

missile A weapon powered by a rocket or jet engine that steers itself toward a target and then explodes.

modified Changed or adapted.

module A section or part of a spacecraft that is joined to other parts of the craft, but may be detached if necessary.

mothership A plane or spacecraft from which a smaller craft is launched.

propeller A device with long, twisted blades that spins fast to move a plane through the air.

radar A system for detecting faraway aircraft by sending out radio waves and listening for any echoes that bounce back from the planes.

rocket A vehicle or engine that works by burning fuel with oxygen to produce a jet of gas that pushes the vehicle through the air. Unlike jet engines, rockets work in space.

satellites Spacecraft that fly around Earth.

seaplane A plane with floats instead of wheels so that it can take off and land on water.

speed of sound The speed at which sound travels through something. The speed of sound in air depends on how warm or cold the air is.

swiveling Turning or rotating.

unmanned Without any person or crew inside.

Notes for parents and teachers

Shape and size

Look through the pictures in the book and talk about why the aircraft are different shapes and sizes. Think about other aircraft that are not included in the book and talk about how they compare to the aircraft shown. Fast jet planes are streamlined. When a jet plane takes off, its wheels fold up inside it and doors close over them. What might happen if the wheels hung down from a plane all the time? Would the plane go faster or slower?

Flying

Birds take off and fly by flapping their wings. Why do you think planes don't have flapping wings? A small plane like the *Bell X-1* rocket-plane weighs about as much as three cars. A large airliner weighs hundreds of tons. How are aircraft that weigh as much as this able to fly when a small pebble weighing a few ounces quickly falls to the ground?

Controls

Talk about how a pilot controls a plane, by using a control stick and rudder pedals to steer the plane and a thrust lever for each engine to make the plane go faster.

Danger

Flying an experimental plane very fast can be dangerous. Talk about how the pilots try to stay safe by wearing a safety harness and a helmet.

Design

Talk about how different types of plane are designed for a particular purpose. For example, airliners are comfortable, with room for passengers and their bags. Cargo planes have lots of space inside. Can you think of other types of plane that are different shapes and sizes? What about business jets and light aircraft?

Drawing

Ask children to draw their own record-breaking plane. What would it look like? What shape would it be? What would it be made of? What sort of engine would it have? How fast do they think it would go? How many people would it carry?